The ABC's of Violin®

for the

Intermediate

Book 2

by

Janice Tucker Rhoda

CARL FISCHER®

65 Bleecker Street, New York, NY 10012

ABC3

Printed in the U.S.A. International copyright secured.

ISBN 0-9663731-1-1

PREFACE

This violin method book is designed for the more advanced student of any age. After many years of combining various methods of teaching both children and adults, I have developed a simple and enjoyable approach for the study of the violin. I use materials which help students advance technically in a gradual, logical and thorough manner. There are short, lyrical warm-up exercises and longer study pieces, as well as familiar classical and poplar melodies. I composed eight of the twenty-four melodies, which fit in perfectly with the development of left-hand and bowing techniques.

To the adult student: I am convinced that I is never too late to begin studying the violin. In fact, adult beginners learn to read music at a very quick pace, have excellent concentration and are highly motivated to practice. Playing the violin is very engaging and the contents of this book are sure to maintain your continued interest.

To the teacher: During my many years of teaching and directing string departments, I dreamed of developing a method that would help beginners of any age feel more at ease and satisfied – a method that would allow them to progress quickly and play precisely, yet learn to read music well. This method book, and the entire series, is designed to fit these criteria.

Here are some key elements to strive for at a lesson:

1. impeccable intonation
2. solid bow technique
3. correct posture
4. steady rhythm
5. accurate reading
6. beautiful tone quality
7. expressive vibrato
8. structured, artistic phrasing
9. precise shifting
10. memorization of pieces*

* Although it is not essential to memorize pieces, as a teacher I have found it to be a very useful tool in developing a student's skill. To paraphrase Rudolf Kolisch (1896-1978), a good memory is a habit formed. His quartet, the Kolisch String Quartet, was the first to perform its works by memory.

In any case, it is wise to help our students develop good habits right from the start.

Teaching students of all ages is very gratifying. I think teachers will have the same positive experience I have had while using the series.

Janice Tucker Rhoda
New England Conservatory of Music Faculty and Alumna

I dedicate this book to my devoted teachers:

Nancy Cirillo, Arturo Delmoni, Alan Hawryluk, Joseph Leary, Rudolf Kolisch,
Yuri Mazurkevich, George Neikrug, Daniel Pinkham, Eric Rosenblith,
Gunther Schuller, Roman Totenberg, and Benjamin Zander.

TABLE of CONTENTS
(Excludes warm-ups)

LESSON 1
SLURS
(a continuation of Book 1)

① Warm-ups

②

The Merry Widow
Waltz

Franz Lehar

③ Moderato

④ Warm-up

Count: 1   2 +

Be sure to look for the Easy Piano Accompaniment for Book 2

Russian Folk Song

(5) Allegro

Ludwig van Beethoven

Syncopation or syncopated rhythm:

The rhythmic accent is on the weak beat (versus the strong beat) of the measure.

Count: 1 + 2 + 3   4   ✳

✳ An accent sign

Turkey In The Straw

The Lost Horizon
Ha-Ofek He-Avud

J.T. Rhoda

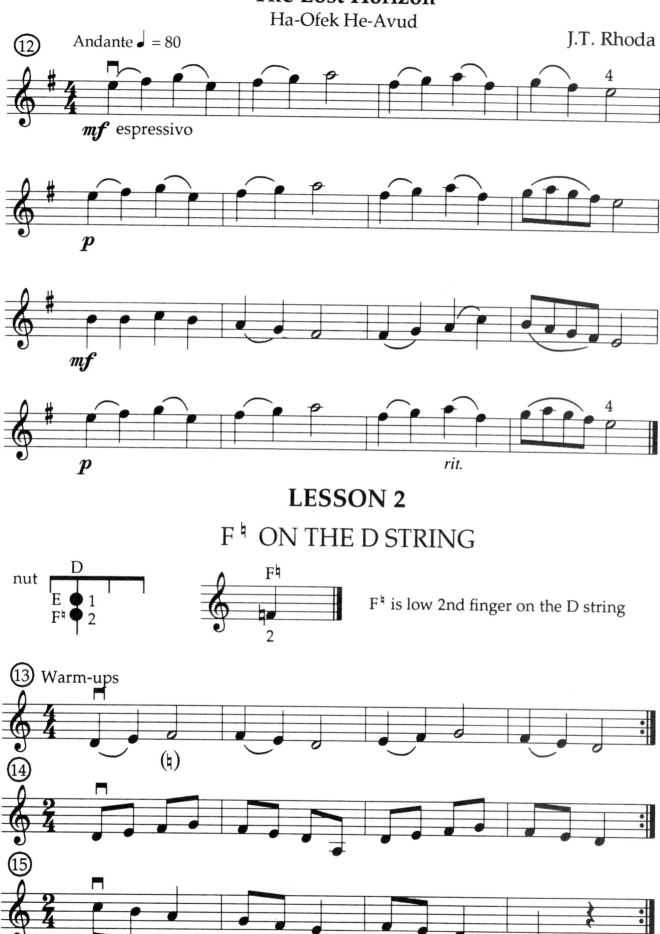

LESSON 2

F♮ ON THE D STRING

F♮ is low 2nd finger on the D string

HANUKA
Holiday Song

Duple time: a time signature with 2 beats per measure (2/4 or 2/2)

In alla breve or "cut time" (¢ = 2/2), there are 2 beats per measure and the half note receives 1 beat.

Cherry Blossoms
Sakura

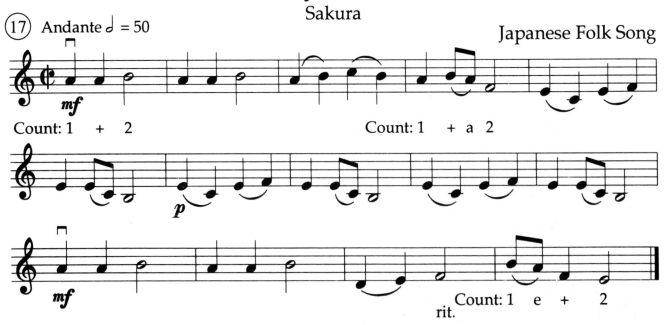

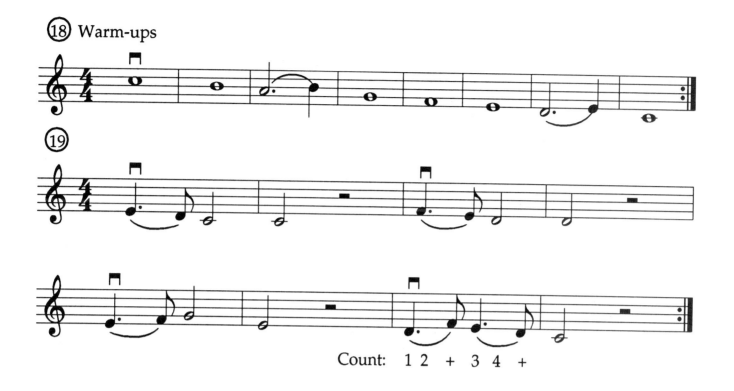

⑱ Warm-ups

⑲

Count: 1 2 + 3 4 +

Country Gardens

⑳ Allegro

English Dance

mf

f

Oats and Beans

Pin The Tail On The Donkey

2nd Verse: He tries to run from me far-ther, he tries to run from me far-ther
But I will soon catch up with him, he has no chance with me.
Oh no, oh no, oh no! He has no chance with me!

Surprise Symphony

24 Andante   Franz Joseph Haydn

mp

mf

poco rit.

mp a tempo

5 means 5 beats per measure.
8 means an eighth note (♪) receives 1 beat.

25 Warm-ups

Count: 1 2 3 4 5   1 2 3 4 5   1 2 3 4 5   1 2 3 4 5

26

1 2 3 4 5

The Native's Chant

27 Adagio ♪ = 69   J.T. Rhoda

p dolce

LESSON 3
G♯ ON THE D STRING

G♯ is high 3rd finger on the D string

Hop Scotch

Moderato ♩ = 100

J.T.Rhoda

The Galway Piper
Rakes of Mallow

Irish Folk Song

C# ON THE G STRING

C# is high 3rd finger on the G string

Early One Morning

36 Allegretto

English Folk Song

mf

(#)

mp

4

pp   *mf*

D♯ ON THE A STRING

nut

A

B 1
C♯ 2
D♯ 3

D♯

D♯ is high 3rd finger on the A string

3

37 Warm-ups

38

Aura Lee

39 Andante

American Folk Song

(#)

LESSON 4

Bb is low 1st finger on the A string

F♮ is low 1st finger on the E string

⑩ Warm-ups

㊶

㊷

Hot Cross Buns

⑬ Moderato   Key of Bb Major   English Folk Song

(♭)

⑭ Moderato   Key of F Major

(♮)

Gentle Breezes
Soyokaze

J.T.Rhoda

㊺ Adagio ♩ = 72

Tourelay
Sweet Betsy From Pike

㊻ Moderato

Dennis O'Shay

Count: 1 2 3 4 5 6 +

㊼ Warm-up

(♭)

Deck The Halls

Auld Lang Syne

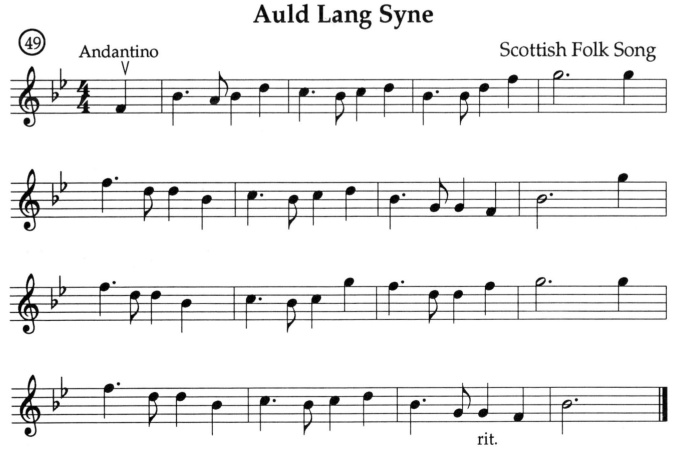

Whistle A Tune

Moderato ♩ = 104

J.T.Rhoda

Count:　1　2　+　3　　4　+

Minuet

2da volta rit.

Beautiful Dreamer

Stephen Foster

Count: 1 2 3 4 5 6   7 8 9

rit.

LESSON 5

There are 3 triplet eighth notes (♪♪♪) in 1 quarter note.

Say: "tri - p - let   tri - p - let"

♪ is a sixteenth note. It receives 1/4 of a beat.

A dotted eighth note (♪.) followed by a sixteenth note (♪) receives 1 beat. $♪. + ♪ = ♩$
$$3/4 + 1/4 = 1$$

57 Warm-ups

Count:　1　e　2　e　1　　2

58

Row Your Boat

59 Allegretto　　　　　　　　　　　　　　　　　American Folk Song

60 Warm-up

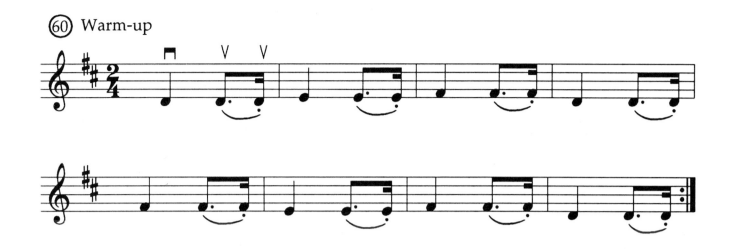

Three Blind Mice

61 Allegro

American Folk Song

Joy To The World

Lowell Mason
after George Frideric Handel

Count: 1   +   2   + a   1   2   + a

LESSON 6

Eb is low 1st finger on the D string

Bb is low 2nd finger on the G string

63 Warm-ups

64

65

66

Amazing Grace

Londonderry Air

Danny Boy

LESSON 7
E♭ ON THE A STRING

E♭ is low 4th finger on the A string

69 Warm-ups

70

71

rhythmic equation:

72 Warm-up

Count: 1   + a 2   + a

Skip To My Lou

73 Allegro

American Folk Song

Count: 1   2   1 + a 2   (♭)

1 + a 2 +

For He's A Jolly Good Fellow

74 Allegretto

English Folk Song

1 2 3 4 5 6

Piano Concerto No. 1

Piotr Ilyich Tchaikovsky

⑦⑤ Lento

appassionato

molto rit.

LESSON 8
3 STUDY PIECES

⑦⑥ Warm-ups

⑦⑦

Gigue Study

Bowing variation: slur 3 notes per bow

J.T. Rhoda

✻ 1——— Keep the 1st finger down while playing the entire measure.

Rock 'n Roll Study

J.T.Rhoda

Study No. 3

Franz Wohlfahrt

LESSON 9
7 MAJOR SCALES

G MAJOR SCALE

D MAJOR SCALE

A MAJOR SCALE

E MAJOR SCALE

C MAJOR SCALE

F MAJOR SCALE

B♭ MAJOR SCALE

LESSON 10
3 MINOR SCALES

A NATURAL MINOR SCALE

D NATURAL MINOR SCALE

E NATURAL MINOR SCALE

Use your metronome at different speeds: ♩ = 50   ♩ = 60   ♩ = 80

Use varied rhythms:

Use varied bowings:

Worksheet

Directions:
1. Write the letter names above the notes.
2. Write the finger numbers below the notes.

_____'s ABCs Practice Chart
Age_____

Lesson-Day Date	Lesson Day							Total Time Practiced This Week	Stars
	Lesson counts: min.							min.	
	Lesson counts: min.							min.	
	Lesson counts: min.							min.	
	Lesson counts: min.							min.	
	Lesson counts: min.							min.	
	Lesson counts: min.							min.	
	Lesson counts: min.							min.	
	Lesson counts: min.							min.	
	Lesson counts: min.							min.	
	Lesson counts: min.							min.	
	Lesson counts: min.							min.	
	Lesson counts: min.							min.	
	Lesson counts: min.							min.	
	Lesson counts: min.							min.	
	Lesson counts: min.							min.	
	Lesson counts: min.							min.	
	Lesson counts: min.							min.	
	Lesson counts: min.							min.	

ABC3

Please Practice Every Day

_____'s ABCs Practice Chart
Age_____

Lesson-Day Date	Lesson Day							Total Time Practiced This Week	Stars
	Lesson counts: min.							min.	
	Lesson counts: min.							min.	
	Lesson counts: min.							min.	
	Lesson counts: min.							min.	
	Lesson counts: min.							min.	
	Lesson counts: min.							min.	
	Lesson counts: min.							min.	
	Lesson counts: min.							min.	
	Lesson counts: min.							min.	
	Lesson counts: min.							min.	
	Lesson counts: min.							min.	
	Lesson counts: min.							min.	
	Lesson counts: min.							min.	
	Lesson counts: min.							min.	
	Lesson counts: min.							min.	
	Lesson counts: min.							min.	
	Lesson counts: min.							min.	
	Lesson counts: min.							min.	

ABC3

Please Practice Every Day